EVERYDAY
I AM JUST
DEAF

KELLINA POWELL

Deaf Queen Boss

To my grandmother, Justa Velinor

My grandma showed me that no matter our

differences we can strive to be whoever we

want to be.

"No limits and believe in yourself because I

do."

New Life

Age four.

I was confused.

I had different hearing.

I will never know what it is like

to have normal hearing.

Normal hearing is dead to me.

Where do I start?

Life is crazy without

hearing. I respect my hearing aid.

Without it, I can't succeed.

Hearing is hard.

Voices are hard to understand.

Can hear very little or

may not hear anything at all.

Is everybody's voice different?

Where is it damaged?

The hair cells in a portion

of the inner ear called the cochlea.

Cochlea, thanks to you

my life has changed.

I feel hopeless.

I sometimes sit in the dark.

Wondering to myself,

Why was I born this way?

Why can't I be like everybody else?

This is not fair!

I never asked to be born this way!

Life's a roller coaster;

you have no control.

The only control you have

is how you react.

Life is empty.

Life can make us stronger than ever.

N ever doubt your strength.

Everybody's life is different.

Strength is key.

Use that strength.

Fight that devil inside you.

No matter what it is,

You can fight it.

Not everything needs a reaction.

Sometimes it is a sign

for us to keep fighting.

Fighting can be tough,

but don't stop.

God gives us a

second language.

Sign language is a

beautiful language.

It's amazing how we can

communicate.

We do not need to be different.

We need to communicate somehow.

I didn't grow up

with sign language

But that doesn't mean

I am different.

I learned to speak and sign.

Anybody can learn it.

Can you hear me?

Hello?

Can't you hear me?

You're dumb!

Wow.

I need to speak to someone else.

Don't treat me differently

because I am deaf.

Hearing people

don't know how

to be nice.

I get anxiety

being around

hearing people.

A lot of stress.

Why can't you be nice?

School is not my favourite place.

Nobody wants to accommodate me.

I will fail school.

My teachers don't care about me.

What can I do? Drop out.

Don't let education fail you.

Study hard.

You need education to get you far.

I am close but I can do it.

I will never allow

no teacher to put me down.

I hate grammar.

I can't spell.

My speech

does not match

with my writing.

My speech is difficult to understand.

I can't pronounce everything correctly.

Why do people use nice people?

I have been used.

Why?

Is it because I have a disability?

I don't get it.

I can't stand hearing people.

Why can't I get far in life?

Why do I need to work

Ten times harder than them?

I've had enough.

I can't get a break.

But a break is never the answer.

I can't hear you.

I need to read your lips.

Face me.

Talk slowly.

Ugh? Why can't you just hear?

This is my life 24/7.

Always reading lips.

Yes, I am a lip reader.

You need to face me when speaking.

I never asked to be born this way.

It's hard on me too.

Self Identity

What is that in your ear?

What the heck,

you can't hear?

How?

Why?

So, you can't hear at all?

So, what happened?

I will tell you when I am ready.

M

y disability doesn't identify

who I am.

I am a strong black woman.

I have a lot of potential.

I am a hustler.

I am caring,

honest,

open-minded, and

loving.

I will not allow anybody

to disrespect me.

I am grateful for you.

I love my hearing aid.

Without you,

I wouldn't be able to hear.

I have up and down days with you.

Do I need a caption?

I don't want people to make fun of me.

Why was I born this way?

I need it to understand

what is going on.

Whatever. I can't hear anyways.

Love

D ating?

No. I am scared.

I don't want to be used.

I can't date hearing people.

I am scared I'll be taken advantage of.

But it doesn't have to be that way.

Dating is beautiful.

Don't be scared to date.

Family.

Without you,

I don't know where I would be.

I wouldn't be strong like you.

I wouldn't build my self-esteem.

Family is in my heart.

Without family,

I wouldn't be

who I am today.

I love you.

Friends.

Without you,

I wouldn't beat school.

Without you,

I wouldn't pass my essay.

Without you,

I wouldn't have my happiness.

Without you,

I wouldn't be annoying.

I love you.

F

amily and friends cheer me up.

Without them,

my life would be boring.

My motivation.

My cheerleaders.

My happiness.

I would be empty without them.

Life of the party.

Partying is fun until you can't hear.

Lights are off.

Deaf people can't hear music.

I can't party and hear music clearly.

Late night.

Having doubts if I will be successful.

Do I still need some resources to help me to

become successful?

Why can't I have it all?

Why do I always need help?

Being deaf is hard.

You get it easy because you're deaf.

You don't need to put in a lot of work.

You can always get help.

No. It is not easy.

I still have to work my butt off.

No matter what I do,

I still need to put in 100% effort.

Recovery

W hy are you always angry?

I am sorry. I can't always

hear if you are not facing me.

Hearing people should be

more educated.

Can't blame them because

school never taught them

how to communicate.

You can drive?

Yes.

I can drive.

I can see.

I am not dead.

Why do people ask

stupid questions?

How do you do it?

I kept my hope and

always prayed.

I have lost two

important people.

I have a family

who is looking up to me.

Stop sending voice notes.

Just text.

I already had a long day

by listening to a lot of voices.

I won't hear everything

because I can't read your lips.

Please. Text.

Let's dance!

Let it all out and scream.

Move your body.

Let that stress go.

I am tired.

I need a break.

Do I want to hear today?

Why can't things be easier

so I can communicate?

I hate school.

No teachers want to help me.

Peers are willing to help but

Notetakers are not the greatest.

Being an entrepreneur and deaf?

There are up and down challenges.

Won't do Zoom calls all the time.

Watching someone

through the screen is enough.

Having a clear screen.

I'm sorry, what?

You can't understand what I'm saying?

No, you have a strong accent.

Why can't I understand accents?

I have to listen really hard.

It is so hard.

What should I do?

Your TV is loud.

Turn it down!

It is not my fault.

I can't hear directly to my ear.

Why can't TVs have Bluetooth?

A Bluetooth hearing aid is expensive.

Treat me like a human being.

I am no different.

No need to be rude.

What makes me different?

I'm deaf.

I am not dead, once again.

R

epeat that again.

Why can't you hear the first time?

Please.

I'm deaf.

I had a rough day.

No.

I'm sorry.

Please.

How do you build self-esteem?

My grandma,

aunt, and

mom.

You are a gift from God.

You are special

in your own unique way.

Never allow anybody to disrespect you.

It's hard to build self-esteem.

You have to remind yourself.

YOU ARE STRONG.

YOU ARE WISE.

YOU ARE BEAUTIFUL.

Never think twice.

Brush it off.

There are still good people out there.

I hate Zoom calls.

Poor connection.

The Internet started to go in and out.

I miss a few words.

I hate Zoom calls.

Being an entrepreneur is hard.

Having to constantly listen.

Some days, I want a break.

Hearing and being

an entrepreneur are hard.

But I want to be wealthy.

I had no idea.

What do you mean?

You wear a hearing aid?

Why didn't you tell me?

I am upset that

you kept that secret from me!

I don't need to tell you if

I don't feel comfortable.

I hid my hearing aid

during the interview.

90% of people with disabilities

do not get hired.

I have never seen or met

a deaf person who works in retail.

I am a hustler and being deaf

doesn't define who I am.

You are beautiful the way you are.

Don't let any man tell you different.

You don't need to settle for less because you

are deaf.

You are beautiful. You are handsome.

You don't need to be an open book.

Be open when you're ready.

No pressure.

Felt comfortable with my hearing

at the age of 20.

You don't know how to spell.

Your grammar is bad

for a university student.

Grammar is important in university.

I don't care.

Grammar is nothing.

I hate grammar.

Why can't we do a video on essays?

Don't let a teacher tell you what to do.

Go chase that dream of yours.

Don't let education stop you

from chasing that dream.

I am graduating from university.

Post-Secondary

Too much workload

I can't keep up.

I can't go to lectures.

It is too big.

Notetakers save me.

Depend on notetakers.

Notetakers and interpreters are gifts.

They are our resources.

Don't disrespect.

I need them to learn.

Leave them alone.

Speaking louder doesn't help.

Talk slower.

Don't be weird moving your lips.

I am a person who can lip read

very well.

It's still a lot of work for my eyes.

A lot of filling in the puzzles.

Guesswork to figure out

what someone was saying.

Deaf is about hearing with your eyes.

I am always watching lips.

It is draining every day.

I am tired.

Do not turn your back on me.

I won't be able to hear everything.

I will be guessing what you're saying.

It's best if you face or look at me.

Side Note

Side note.

Not all deaf people lip read.

Not all deaf people can sign.

I cannot sign.

I was never taught.

I did when I was in grade one.

I

f you see me as a deaf person.

Screw you.

I'm more than just my disability.

I am strong.

I am wise.

I am a queen.

I am a boss.

Why don't you be a nurse?

I said, I wanted to be a doctor.

But it's a long way.

I think you should reconsider.

Just because I am deaf

doesn't mean I can't do it.

There are deaf doctors in the U.S.

Don't allow teachers

to tell you differently.

You can achieve any goal you want!

Captions are important.

I don't care.

I need it.

Finally, my voice is heard.

I got my captions.

The only thing I can't do is hear.

I can drive.

I can listen to music.

I have a life.

Be mindful.

No, my parents are not deaf.

Nobody in my family is deaf.

There is no genetic problem

that involves hearing.

I am a gift.

I am the only one who is deaf.

D
inner table.

I can't keep up with everybody.

I choose not to talk.

It's hard to focus.

You don't look deaf.

You're too pretty to be deaf.

What is deaf supposed to look like?

There is no way to look deaf.

Deaf people are beautiful.

Do not judge.

W

hy do you speak like that?

Instead of getting offended,

I educate people.

I tell them that I am deaf.

Every deaf person's speech is different.

I am here to prove that

deaf people can do anything.

Do what you want to do.

It is different for us.

Yes, we may need accommodation.

But it doesn't mean anything.

Stop saying never mind.

I didn't hear the first time.

I didn't get to hear it.

Repeat.

Please.

Please.

I sign too!

I do not sign. Thank you.

Don't just guess.

Ask.

I don't like

when people think

I need to sign.

Deaf people can talk?

Do not be surprised if

some deaf people do.

Not everyone can.

Be mindful.

Why don't you get a cochlear

implant?

It is an option but

it is not for everybody.

Not everyone wants to hear.

Not everyone wants to give up their identity

for equipment.

Everybody is different.

I'm sorry.

Why are you saying sorry?

You didn't create me.

I am proud I am deaf.

Hey! Being deaf is not a bad thing.

I turn off my hearing aid

when I am annoyed.

Best feeling ever!

Enter a realm of total silence.

Keep in mind.

Not all sign languages are the same.

Every country signs differently.

Be careful how you approach.

"How do you do it? I would kill myself."

Don't ever say that.

We never asked to be born this way.

Be grateful for what you have.

Can you multitask?

Deafness does not equal

learning disabilities.

Those are two different things.

Do not mistake deafness for

learning disabilities.

We can still achieve anything

even if we are deaf.

If you are not patient,

It won't go anywhere.

If you can't repeat your words twice,

We will not work out.

You need to be patient.

Celebration

We deserve respect.

We are human.

Deafness does not equal

a learning disability.

We do not need

to be shut out of the world.

We've had enough.

Include us like a normal human.

Respect us deaf women.

We've had men take advantage

of us before.

Deaf women have a voice.

We will speak in our own voice.

I

don't get it.

Why is dating hard?

Dating a hearing person can be hard.

But it doesn't mean it won't work out.

Not all hearing people are rude.

You just need to find the ones

who are mindful.

Education is key.

Don't be afraid of telling them

what your needs are.

Coach yourself.

Value yourself.

Self-talk is important.

Accept your flaws.

How can you hear from your phone?

Bluetooth!

Technology has grown a lot.

I am overwhelmed

with how technology has grown.

Take out the hearing aid.

Ultimate relaxation.

Perfect sleep!

Sink into a world of silence.

Long day at work.

My eyes are tired.

I just want to sleep.

My eyes are my ears.

Why isn't there a caption?

I don't understand!

Isn't it a movie theatre?!

Cimplex, what are you doing

for those who can't hear?

Do better!

How much is it?

Hearing aid batteries

are expensive

but why?

We never asked to be born this way.

Gosh damn it.

I see you at an event

and there's no batteries on you.

Hearing slowly dying.

Wouldn't it be a shame

if I just Died?

Why do hearing people do that to us?

It's been lovely.

I am now

turning off

my hearing aids.

See you in the next book.

ABOUT THE AUTHOR

 KELLINA POWELL
the Deaf Queen Boss.

At the age of four she lost
100% of her hearing in both
ears and on a journey to
overcome many challenges living in a hearing
world. Nothing can stop her from doing what she
wants from playing basketball, soccer, and Rugby
in the States to getting her bachelor's degree in
Psychology from York University and her
post-graduate certificate in Mental Health and
Addiction.

Based out of Toronto, Canada Kellina is changing
the future for young professionals with disabilities,
showing them that they can have the life they
desire and accomplish their goals. As an advocate
for people with disabilities, Kellina has appeared
in over two dozen podcasts in five countries. To
learn more about how you can become an ally in
the deaf community, visit
www.youtube.com/c/deafqueenboss.

Kellina Powell is a gift to our world. She has proven that no matter what obstacles are in her way, she can overcome them. As a deaf person living in a hearing world, she gives us a peek behind the curtain for living with a disability and creating a life she loves.

In her first book, *Everyday I am Just Deaf*, Kellina exposes her inner thoughts and feelings to get readers thinking:

- what it's like to be deaf in a hearing world
- what barriers can be removed and
- what contributions can be made to level the playing field.

Kellina shares her journey so we can better understand how to be a more inclusive world and the considerations that hearing people can make to change the world for people with disabilities.

Made in the USA
Columbia, SC
31 May 2022